Vanishing Wetlands

Look for these and other books in the Lucent
Overview series:

Vanishing Wetlands

by Anita Louise McCormick

OUR ENDANGERED PLANET

LUCENT *Overview Series*

LUCENT Overview Series

Library of Congress Cataloging-in-Publication Data

McCormick, Anita Louise.
    Vanishing wetlands / by Anita Louise McCormick.
       p.   cm. — (Lucent overview series)
    Includes bibliographical references and index.
    ISBN 1-56006-162-6 (acid free)
    1. Wetland ecology—Juvenile literature.   2. Wetland conserva-
tion—Juvenile literature.   3. Wetlands—Juvenile literature. [1.
Wetlands. 2. Wetland ecology. 3. Ecology. 4. Conservation of
natural resources.] I. Title. II. Series.
  QH541.5.M3M42   1995
  574.5'26325—dc20   94-27653
                                                            CIP
                                                             AC

© Copyright 1995 by Lucent Books, Inc.
P.O. Box 289011, San Diego, CA 92198-9011
Printed in the U.S.A.

Contents

1

A Misunderstood Resource

WETLANDS HAVE BEEN misunderstood throughout much of human history. They have been the subject of superstition and legend. They have inspired stories of evil spirits and monsters. Such tales may have developed because of the many strange and wondrous creatures that dwell in wetlands. Snakes, lizards, insects, and alligators can all be found in wetlands of one type or another. One folk legend, known in the swampy Tombigbee River region of Alabama as "Wiley and the Hairy Man," warns of a hairy monster that kidnaps children who venture too close to the swamp.

The fear of disease

Legend and superstition are not the only basis for longstanding fears about wetlands. People long ago noticed a connection between wetland areas and disease. As far back as the first century, Lucius Junius Columella, a Roman agricultural expert and writer, advised European farmers not to build near a swamp "which breeds insects armed with annoying stings . . . and crawling things deprived of their winter moisture and infected with poison by mud and decaying filth,

(Opposite page) A close look at a swamp reveals why it is the stuff of legend and superstition. Even in daylight, a swamp seems full of mystery.

from which are often contracted mysterious diseases." The unusual, sometimes unpleasant odor commonly detected around wetlands—especially swampy wetlands—probably added to Columella's concern about "decaying filth." What Columella and others for some time after him did not know is that the odor had nothing to do with filth. It is produced as plants and other organic materials are broken down by bacteria during the natural process of decay.

The connection between wetlands and disease was real, however, even if it was misunderstood. Malaria, yellow fever, and other terrible diseases were common around some swamps and marshes, especially those located in tropical and semitropical areas. These diseases were especially hard on European settlers. Unlike the native populations of tropical countries, the settlers had no natural immunity to the diseases.

Fears for public health prompted campaigns to eliminate swamps and other wetland areas. The American Public Health Association took an active role in these campaigns. In 1876 the organization's president said, "The [government] cannot afford to be indifferent to the presence of swamps because they check [halt] production, limit population and reduce the standard of health and vigor."

Eliminating mosquitoes

By the late 1800s doctors began to realize that it was not the swamps but the mosquitoes living and breeding in the swamps that were transmitting the feared diseases. Dr. Ronald Ross, a British physician who was awarded the Nobel Prize for medicine for his work, proved in 1897 that malaria spreads as a result of mosquito bites. Scientists later discovered that malaria is carried by about sixty species of mosquitoes that live in tropical and semitropical regions of the world.

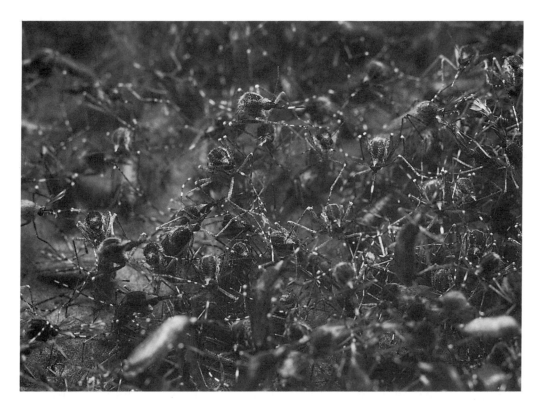

Several other serious diseases, including yellow fever and encephalitis, are also transmitted by insects and other small animals that live in some tropical and semitropical wetlands.

Once the connection between mosquitoes and disease was made, the drive to drain and fill wetlands expanded. Mosquitoes lay their eggs in almost any size body of still water, so this meant eliminating swamps, marshes, ponds, and even small puddles of standing water. In 1890 Dr. Ross traveled to Freetown, Sierra Leone, in western Africa and set to work in an attempt to drain every puddle large enough for the breeding of malaria-carrying mosquitoes. In a letter to a colleague in Great Britain, Ross described his strategy for ridding Freetown of mosquitoes:

> We all agree that if the local authorities will set themselves to the task, Freetown can be free of

The federal campaign to eliminate wetlands gathered steam once scientists realized that disease-carrying mosquitoes bred in wetland areas.

insects at a trifling cost. We carefully made a map of the whole town locating all the Anopheles [a malaria-carrying species of mosquito] puddles. . . . They could all be drained at little cost and most could be swept out with a broom.

Dr. Malcolm Watson, a British physician who had read Dr. Ross's ideas on malaria, went to the town of Kelang, Malaysia, to launch a similar drive in 1901. At the time of his arrival nearly all of the small town's population of thirty-five hundred were ill with malaria. He immediately decided that a twenty-two-acre swamp, which was located in the middle of the town, should be drained and filled. This pattern of draining and filling swamps, marshes, and other wetland areas occurred over and over in tropical and semitropical areas around the world. Doctors and scientists hoped their efforts would rid the world of mosquito-borne diseases.

Since it is virtually impossible to remove all sources of water that are suitable for mosquito breeding in any area, the spread of malaria could be slowed, but not stopped. Today, even after countless wetlands have been destroyed in the fight against malaria, the disease persists. More than 100 million people worldwide contract malaria each year and more than one million die of the disease annually, the journal *Economist* reported in October 1992.

In the name of progress

The draining and filling of wetlands continues to be a common practice, although concern about public health is no longer the major reason for this activity. Researchers estimate that more than half of the world's wetlands have been destroyed or severely damaged. Some states in the United States—California, Indiana, Illinois, Iowa, Missouri, Kentucky, and Ohio—have lost more than

80 percent of their wetlands. Much of this destruction has been caused by the requirements of urban development and farming. Rivers and streams feeding into wetlands have been rerouted and the wetlands themselves drained and filled, or reduced in size.

These changes have often been made in the name of progress. Wetlands, thought to have no real value in their natural state, were seen as having greater financial and land-use potential in some other form. Many people today still do not understand exactly what a wetland is and why it is so valuable. At its simplest, a wetland is an area of ground that is covered by shallow water, where the water level constantly rises and falls. The lack of understanding about wetlands is not really surprising, considering past attitudes and the unique characteristics of wetlands themselves.

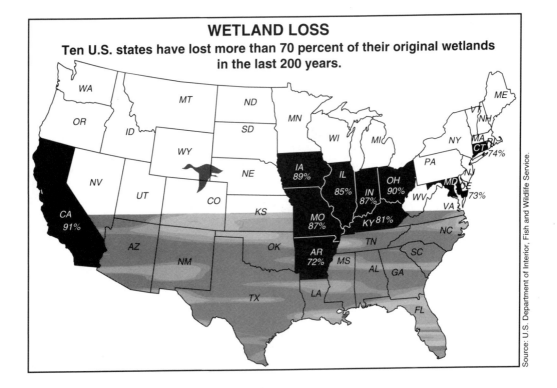

WETLAND LOSS

Ten U.S. states have lost more than 70 percent of their original wetlands in the last 200 years.

Source: U.S. Department of Interior, Fish and Wildlife Service.

Many wetlands are quiet, subtle places. They can extend for miles or appear to be little more than large puddles in the middle of fields. But an observer who watches long enough may see flocks of migrating ducks and geese gathering there, flapping their wings and dipping their heads beneath the water's surface in search of small fish or other tasty food. For these birds a wetland in an otherwise dry area is an oasis—a place where they can find food and water and rest for a while before they continue on their journey.

These wetlands are especially important to waterfowl, who stop at them during their annual migration to eat, drink, and raise their young. When wetlands are destroyed, the waterfowl population declines. Roger L. DiSilvestro, former senior editor of *Audubon* magazine, says:

> In all, before European settlers took over development of the continent from the forces of nature, waterfowl in the lower 48 states had more than 200 million acres of wetlands in which to court,

This black-necked stilt is just one of many birds who lives in a wetland habitat. Even today, many people do not understand the delicate wetland ecosystem.

feed and nest, an area more than four times the size of New York State. These marshes, prairie potholes, swamps, bogs, and coastal salt marshes produced not only waterfowl, but some five thousand plant species, 190 species of amphibians, and a third of all the birds in the United States.

Waterfowl thrive in Houron Marsh. Such wetlands provide important homes for waterfowl.

A difficult balance

The struggle to protect wetlands often puts environmentalists at odds with farm groups and commercial developers as to how much protection they should be given. Disagreements between those who believe protecting wetlands should have the highest legal priority and farmers and commercial developers who feel it should be their right to use their property as they see fit have led to many long and complicated legal

Cypress trees grow side by side in a thriving South Carolina wetland. Determining how much protection wetlands should receive is often a source of controversy between environmentalists and developers.

battles. Each side of this debate tries to convince lawmakers at the federal, state, and local levels of government that its position on wetland regulation is correct.

Government agencies, judges, and other officials are put in the position of trying to determine how to best protect wetlands while still allowing for reasonable use whenever possible. This is a difficult task because some kinds of wetlands can tolerate more use than others and still maintain their value as functioning wetlands. Environmental writer G. Tyler Miller Jr. says:

> It is difficult to protect these lands while trying to allow for reasonable use. There are many different kinds of wetlands and plans for protecting one kind may not work for another. There is tremendous political and economic pressure to over-use

wetlands. Plans for controlled use of wetlands
[are] hampered by the conflicting goals of many
coastal municipalities, counties and states.

Scientists still have much to learn about wetlands. While some wetlands are able to withstand
a limited amount of misuse and still thrive, other
similar wetland ecosystems are destroyed much
more easily. This often makes it difficult for lawmakers to determine exactly how much protection
a particular wetland area requires, as well as how
much protection wetlands need in general.

Laws have now been passed in many parts of
the world to stop wetland destruction. But the future of these valuable ecosystems is still at stake.
The survival of wetland ecosystems throughout
the world depends on several factors. Among the
most important are the continued government
protection of wetlands, stricter enforcement of
wetland protection laws, and increasing the public's awareness of the wetlands' value.

2

Life in the Wetlands

WETLANDS ARE FULL of life. Each wetland is an individual ecosystem, a community of plants and animals that depend on each other to obtain what they need for survival. The wet areas of a wetland support many insects, tiny fish, and fairy shrimp. These creatures provide food for larger animals such as turtles, fish, and birds that live in the wetland habitat. Wetlands also attract ducks, geese, and other migratory birds that stop to eat the fish and grain and other plants that wetlands provide in abundance. Some wetlands are home to very large animals. The largest living reptile on the North American continent, the alligator, can be found in wetlands in the southern United States. Large or small, every plant and every animal that lives in a wetland plays an important role in the chain of life of that ecosystem.

A unique environment

About 6 percent of the world's landmass is made up of wetlands. Wetlands can be found in diverse regions, ranging from the frozen wilderness of Alaska to the tropical band that hugs the equator. The continental United States has about seventy million acres of wetlands; every state in

(Opposite page) A majestic blue heron dominates the marsh as he searches for his morning meal. Consisting of 6 percent of the world's landmass, wetlands provide valuable homes for many water animals.

The Florida alligator, the largest living reptile in North America, can only thrive in a wetland environment.

the country has at least one type of wetland. Some of the world's wetlands are found near oceans, some along rivers and streams, and others on inland prairies. Most wetlands consist of freshwater. In the United States, for example, 94 percent of wetlands are freshwater wetlands. But there are also saltwater wetlands and brackish water wetlands, where saltwater and freshwater meet.

The vegetation in wetlands can be mossy, grassy, shrublike, or wooded. The vegetation found in a wetland helps determine its type. There are many different types of wetlands, including bogs, marshes, swamps, prairie potholes, and wetland forests. Reeds, cattails, and other grasslike plants commonly grow in marshes, for example; trees, bushes, and woody-stemmed plants are most often found in swamps.

Most of the plants in any wetland are aquatic plants that do not normally grow on dry land. This is because water-saturated soil like that found in wetlands lacks the atmospheric gases that most dryland plants need for growth. Cattails, saw grass, and reeds, which are all commonly found in wetlands, require soil that has been soaked underwater for long periods. This type of soil is known as hydric soil.

Some common characteristics

Despite all of their differences, wetlands share some common characteristics, such as shallow water levels. Lynn M. Stone, author of *Wetlands*, says, "Wetlands defy a single or simple definition. They exist in many forms and many locations. All of them share, however, a bond: they are places where the ground is covered by shallow water."

Wetlands also share another characteristic: constantly changing water levels. Sometimes wetlands overflow with water. Other times, especially during the late summer, fall, and winter months, some wetlands become completely dry. Wetlands usually have their highest water level during the spring. The combined effects of melting snow and heavy spring rain cause wetlands to become much larger and wetter in the spring than they are during the dryer part of the year. The fluctuating water level in wetlands is part of what makes wetland ecosystems so unique.

Many kinds of life

Wetland ecosystems are among the world's most biodiverse, meaning that they are able to support a large number of plant and animal species. Many wetlands are comparable to rain forests and coral reefs in the variety of plant and animal species that they are able to support. In

This saw grass can only thrive in a wetland because it requires soil that has been soaked in water for long periods.

the United States alone, over 5,000 species of plants, 270 species of birds, and 190 species of amphibians depend on wetland ecosystems. Wetlands are also home to many endangered plants and animals that could not exist without them. Forty-five percent of North America's endangered animals and 26 percent of its endangered plants are dependent in one way or another on wetland ecosystems.

An astounding number of species of plants and animals can be found in a single wetland. In one survey taken by the U.S. Fish and Wildlife Service, a single, unnamed wetland was found to support 700 different species of plants and animals. That number included 489 species of plants, 126 of birds, 21 of mammals, 12 of reptiles, and numerous species of microscopic life-forms.

Wetlands are prime breeding grounds for waterfowl. Every year ducks, geese, and many other birds use wetlands—especially marshes and prairie potholes—for hatching and raising their

A mallard hen and her young feed along the edge of a wetland marsh. Wetlands are comparable to rain forests in the thousands of species they support.

young. Wetlands supply shelters for their nests, as well as food and water for their young. Marine animals such as shrimp and crabs also use coastal wetlands as hatcheries. Wetlands are important to a wide variety of land animals as well. Raccoons, bears, and wildcats come to the edge of wetlands in search of food and water. While these animals do not actually live in wetlands, they nevertheless need wetland resources for the species to survive.

Wet and dry seasons

Adaptation is the key to survival in the wetlands. The plants, animals, and microorganisms, or organisms of microscopic size, that live in wetland environments must be able to adapt to the changing wet and dry conditions. Some animals live through the dry periods by going into a kind of semihibernation called estivation. An animal in estivation goes into a prolonged light sleep and is able to preserve much of the moisture in its body. Alligators living in swamp wetlands survive dry periods by digging holes deep in the mud, where they can live until the rains return. Other small swamp animals, such as frogs, turtles, water snails, and fish also burrow into alligator holes for protection against the drought. Some of the animals that come here for protection become food for the alligator. Many species of frogs and turtles are able to survive dry periods by digging burrows of their own in the moist mud.

Some wetland animals are not able to survive through the dry season. Many fish and other water-dependent animals die before the rainy season raises the water level again. But enough of these animals usually survive the drought to reproduce, insuring that their species survive. During dry seasons many wetland plants also die. But their seeds, which remain in the wetland soil all winter, sprout when the rains arrive.

A deer takes a backward glance before bounding into the thick vegetation of the Florida Everglades. Although deer do not live in the wetlands, they depend on wetlands for water and food.

The mudflats in Jamaica Bay Wildlife Refuge in New York are home to these periwinkle snails, who will have to go into a state of semihibernation once the water in the mudflats dries up.

During the rainy season the high water levels often cause several small wetland areas to be connected together. They also connect wetlands with nearby bodies of water, such as rivers, streams, ponds, and oceans. When this happens, animals, small plants and plant materials, microorganisms, sediment, nutrients, and other materials flow from one body of water into another. This interchange of materials adds to the wetlands' biodiversity. The materials transported in this way fertilize wetland plants and provide food for wetland animals. High-water periods also distribute seeds of wetland plants from one wetland to another.

The web of life

Every species of plant and animal living in a wetland has a place in the wetland ecosystem's food chain. This position is known as its ecological niche. Most wetland areas are large enough to support more than one ecological niche. This means that plants and animals that require slightly different things from their environment can make the same wetland area their home.

Even small wetland areas usually support more than one ecological niche. The outer rim of a wetland, for example, may support a semiaquatic niche of plants and animals that require only a partially wet environment. The deeper waters near the wetland's center may support plants and animals that require a fully aquatic environment. Edward Maltby, a geography expert at the University of Exeter in Great Britain, says:

> Wetlands exhibit an enormous diversity according to their genesis [origin], geographical location, . . . and chemistry, dominant plants, soil or sediment characteristics. There may be considerable variation within a single wetland area, due to the importance of even subtle differences in flooding. Many types of wetlands can be found in close proximity, forming not just different ecosystems, but wholly distinctive landscapes.

Environmental niches

The larger a wetland area is, the wider the variety of ecological niches it is likely to be able to support. Extremely large wetlands, such as the Florida Everglades, contain several different types of wetlands and a great number of individual environmental niches. The Everglades are made up mostly of swamps. But the Everglades also contain many sections of pine forests, hardwood forests, and regions of semiaquatic and dryland plants. Each environmental niche of the Everglades is home to a select group of plants and animals that rely on the natural features of a given area for survival. And every form of life in all the ecological niches of the Everglades has an important role to play in the ecosystem's food chain.

Even when plants and animals die in a wetland, their role in the ecosystem does not end. Their remains sink into the mud to decay or decompose. Then, as decomposed organic matter, they become the first link in the food chain of the plants,

An American bullfrog stares out from behind a sedge in a marsh. Frogs play a large role in the marsh ecosystem.

animals, and microorganisms that live in the wetland. This keeps the wetland ecosystem supplied with the nutrients it needs to remain healthy.

Marshes

Marshes are among the most common forms of wetland ecosystems in the world. In the continental United States over 90 percent of the wetland areas are marshes. Marshes often resemble watery meadows because many of the plants that grow in them are grasslike in appearance. Cattails, reeds, and other wild grasses all thrive in marshes. Marshes can be found along the coast, near rivers and streams, as well as inland. Some marshes are freshwater, while others are saltwater.

Marshes are home to a diverse variety of wildlife. Birds, fish, frogs, turtles, and many types of aquatic and semiaquatic insects can be found in or around nearly every marsh. Many kinds of animals that are not ordinarily thought of as marsh animals also depend on marsh ecosystems for food. While they live on dry land, they come to the edge of the marsh to eat and drink.

This tidal marsh in Washington County, Maine, is home to a wide variety of plant and animal life. Marshes are the most prevalent wetland in the world.

Osprey hatchlings await their parents. The osprey, or fish hawk, uses the wetlands as its primary source of food.

Sheila Cowling, author of *Our Wild Wetlands*, says, "Raccoons, opossums, snakes and skunks invade the marsh from outside in search of clams, crabs or birds' eggs. An osprey, also called a fish hawk, circles above the grass, searching for crabs, mice and baby birds."

Kushiro Marsh is one of the largest remaining natural wetlands in Japan. This marsh is located in the floodplain of the Kushiro and Akan Rivers. It is an important breeding area for the endangered red-crowned crane. Ducks, geese, swans, and shorebirds also depend on the Kushiro Marsh for food, water, and nesting grounds. In 1935 the Japanese government recognized the importance of this wetland and designated it as an area worthy of special protection. It has also been listed as a national monument.

Prairie potholes

Prairie potholes are small marshes that were carved out by Ice Age glaciers over twelve thousand years ago. In North America they can be found in the midwestern United States and in three Canadian provinces. Prairie potholes vary in size from one-fifth of an acre to twenty-five acres. They usually hold water for several months of the year. Prairie potholes are home to a wide

Prairie potholes were carved out by Ice Age glaciers over twelve thousand years ago. Today, they are frequently eliminated by farmers who drain them to use the water for crops.

variety of wildlife. They are extremely important to ducks, geese, and other migrating waterfowl that make the trip between Canada and the southern United States every year. These waterfowl use prairie potholes as places to rest, eat, and hatch their young.

Over half of the original twenty million acres of prairie pothole wetlands in North America's midwestern region have been drained for agricultural use. The destruction of prairie pothole wetlands causes particularly severe problems for waterfowl during years when the rainfall level is below normal. The drought of 1988 was especially hard on waterfowl. Rain levels were so low during the summer of 1988 that approximately 40 percent of the prairie potholes in the United States and Canada dried up. The U.S. Fish and Wildlife Service discovered that only sixty-six million ducks were able to make the annual migration through North America. This was the second lowest duck migration on record. (The migrating duck population numbered about ninety million in 1980.) It was only surpassed by the severe prairie pothole evaporation rate caused by the extreme droughts, known as the Dust Bowl, that hit the plains states over sixty years ago. U.S. Fish and Wildlife Service director Frank Dunkle said of the 1988 drought, "It's the worst time in the history of waterfowl other than the 1930s."

Swamps

In contrast to the open, watery meadows of marshes and prairie potholes, swamps are often thought of as being dark and mysterious places. They are characterized by algae, moss, vines, and trees and other woody vegetation. The water in swamps is often brown, due to the organic acid that is produced when plants decompose in the water. The plant growth in swamps can be so dense that it is difficult, if not sometimes impossible, to navigate even a small boat through it. The water is often green with clumps of floating plants, and long strands of moss hang down from the trees. The Everglades are among the best-known swamps in North America. Mangrove trees, which are one of the few kinds of trees that

Mangrove trees create a forest-like effect in the swamps of the Everglades.

are able to grow in the salty coastal waters, have tall, stiltlike roots that often extend far above the waterline. Snakes, lizards, turtles, frogs, and fish can be found in abundance. And fish-eating birds can often be seen diving into the water in search of a meal.

Swamps, such as the Everglades, are teeming with many kinds of plant and animal life. They have one of the highest levels of biodiversity of any ecosystem on earth. And all of the elements work together to keep the swamp ecosystem thriving. Jean Craighead George, author of *Everglades Wiseguide*, says:

> Every plant, every physical element is involved in the web of life—as a soil builder, predator, plant-eater, scavenger, agent of decay, or converter of energy and raw materials into food. Damage of or removal of any of these components could destroy the glades as we know them.

Forested wetlands

While swamps support mangroves and other trees that can tolerate having their root systems wet for extended periods, the drier wetlands support many species of trees that are usually found on dry land. Pine and many other types of trees are often found in forested wetland ecosystems. These trees do not grow directly in the standing water, but on raised ridges of soil in or near the wetland. The ground in these dry areas is often covered with plants such as Virginia creeper vines, ferns, and touch-me-nots. The plants that grow in the portions of wetland forests that are continually saturated with water are similar to those that grow in marshes, swamps, or bogs.

Forested wetlands can sometimes be found in the bottomlands, or low-lying lands, near oceans, rivers, and streams. They serve as a winter home for many kinds of waterfowl. The forested wetlands in the lower Mississippi Valley are the win-

tering grounds for most of America's mallard duck population. They also serve as a winter home to nearly all of the wood ducks that migrate through the central part of the United States. These wood ducks depend heavily on forested wetlands because they require the hollow trees these wetlands furnish for nesting sites. They also provide a habitat for many other kinds of wildlife and are an important spawning ground for numerous species of fish. But this vital wildlife habitat is quickly shrinking. Only 25 percent of the original forested wetlands remain in the lower Mississippi Valley. Where there were once over twenty-five million acres of periodically flooded bottomland hardwood forests in the area, only about five million acres remain today. Most of this loss is

Wood ducks depend heavily on wetlands for winter homes and for hollow trees, which are the wood ducks' preferred nesting places.

the result of agricultural drainage. A U.S. Fish and Wildlife Service publication, *America's Endangered Wetlands*, states, "Even today, these remnants are shrinking as tracts are leveled, drained and converted for . . . farming."

Bogs

Like prairie potholes, bogs developed mainly in the depressions left by the retreating glaciers after the Ice Age. But while prairie potholes are full of water throughout much of the year, bogs usually appear to be relatively dry. People who walk across a bog often discover the surface to be soft and spongy. This is because bogs are made up mostly of sphagnum moss and other soft, partially decayed materials. These organic materials are able to absorb and hold large amounts of water like a sponge. Through the centuries mosses and other plant materials accumulate in bogs and gradually decompose. This partially decomposed plant material is known as peat. Many peat deposits ranging from twenty to forty feet deep have been found. Scientists estimate that peat lands cover about 3 percent of the earth's surface. They cover vast areas in Canada, northern Europe, and northern Asia and can be found in smaller quantities in many other parts of the world.

Bog soil usually has a high acid content, so only a limited number of plant species can grow in a bog. Bogs are home to grasses, mosses, and small shrubs such as leatherleaf and poison sumac. They also support some species of wildflowers, including lady's slippers and other orchids. Many of the plants that grow in bog wetlands are classified as threatened or endangered because they are able to grow in so few places in the world. Venus's-flytraps are among the best known of the bog-dwelling plants. At one time Venus's-flytraps grew in bogs in twenty-one countries. Now they can only be found in sixty-five locations in eleven countries. Venus's-flytraps grow best in areas between the shrubby vegetation of bogs and surrounding pine woods. Many people find them fascinating because they are able to catch flies, ants, and other insects in the sticky substance found in their pods. Venus's-flytrap plants must absorb the nitrogen and other materials these insects contain to fulfill their nutritional needs.

A dwindling supply of Venus's-flytraps

Because of their declining supply, Venus's-flytrap plants are protected by law. But the popularity of these plants has created enough of a demand for Venus's-flytraps that poachers are willing to risk arrest to illegally remove them from bogs. The bog wetlands in North Carolina once had an abundant supply of Venus's-flytrap plants, but they are quickly disappearing. In the March/April 1994 issue of *Audubon*, North Carolina Wildlife Resources Commission enforcement officer Milton McLean says, "Used to be, every wooded [bog] area you went to, all over Brunswick County, there would be lots of them. Now there's none."

The same situation exists in many other areas. The World Wildlife Fund, an environmental organization, estimates that 1.1 million flytraps are sold as houseplants in North America annually, and nearly the same number are being shipped to overseas markets. Environmentalists do not know for sure how many of these plants are legally propagated, or produced, from tissue cultures in nurseries and how many plants and bulbs are illegally taken from bogs by poachers. It is only known that the world's supply of Venus's-flytraps

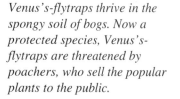

Venus's-flytraps thrive in the spongy soil of bogs. Now a protected species, Venus's-flytraps are threatened by poachers, who sell the popular plants to the public.

is quickly declining, and little is being done to prevent it. In the same issue of *Audubon*, Bruce McBryde of the U.S. Fish and Wildlife Service says, "Eventually, I think Venus flytraps will be more of a natural artifact, preserved only in managed areas."

Compared to other types of wetlands, bogs support few forms of animal life. Nearly all bogs, however, are home to insects such as beetles, dragonflies, and mosquitoes. They are also home to birds, which come to eat these insects. Some types of reptiles and amphibians live in bogs as well. The bog turtle, one of the rarest species of turtles in North America, lives in bogs and swamps from North Carolina to New York.

While the benefits wetland ecosystems furnish to plants and animals are important, that is only part of the reason they should be preserved. Since the beginning of civilization humans have also depended on wetland resources.

3

The Importance of Wetlands

THE RELATIONSHIP BETWEEN wetlands and human civilization dates back thousands of years. Some of the earliest known human settlements, including those of prehistoric cultures in Europe and North America, were built around wetlands. Wetlands provided human communities with food and water and a wide variety of plant materials used for tools, cloth and basket weaving, and building shelters. Edward Maltby, of the University of Exeter in Great Britain, says:

> Wetlands have played a crucial role in human history. . . . Some of the first prehistoric cultures, such as those of the early Mesolithic settlements around the post-glacial lake margins and coasts of Europe and those of the coastal Indian communities in North America, depended on wetlands for food and materials for building, shelter and clothing.

Evidence of an ancient dependence

In the past few centuries archaeologists and anthropologists have found evidence of ancient wetland-dependent communities in many parts of the world. They have uncovered ancient human bodies, bones, and artifacts. Some of the most impressive finds have occurred in bogs. Bodies

(Opposite page) Tourists learn about a wetland area in Elkhorn Slough, California. Wetlands were important resources to early man, providing building materials for shelters.

found in bogs were particularly well preserved because bogs generally have a high acid content and are low in oxygen, making it difficult for bacteria and other microorganisms to break down organic matter. Even some of the clothes, woven from wetland-grown fibers, were preserved on many bodies discovered in bogs. The first of these bodies was discovered in 1773 in a peat bog at Rawnholt, Denmark, by a worker who was digging peat. Through the years, over 2,000 bodies have been found in the wetland bogs of Europe. They are estimated to have died between 800 B.C. and A.D. 400. Over 160 bodies, estimated to be over seven thousand years old, have also been discovered in a wetland bog at Windover, Florida.

By studying these bodies and the tools, clothing, and other items buried with them or found nearby, anthropologists have gained a better understanding of how early cultures were able to use the many resources that wetlands provided in their daily lives. The preserved items they found included food, cloth, cooking utensils, and weapons. Many of these ancient artifacts were made from wetland plants. Others were made from the bones of animals that lived in wetland areas.

Third World communities

Even today wetlands continue to play a crucial role in the lives of many communities. This is especially true in Third World or developing nations, where rural and tribal people living near wetlands meet nearly all their needs with wetland resources. Wetlands provide them with a place to grow and hunt food. Wetlands also provide them with numerous kinds of plant materials for building, weaving cloth and baskets, and other needs. Wetlands also act as reservoirs for the groundwater supply, preventing community wells from going dry.

A man rows in front of his marsh house in Iraq. In Third World nations, wetlands provide villagers with nearly all of their daily needs for survival.

Wetland-dependent communities are especially common in the Third World nations in Africa, Asia, and Latin America. In these communities life is built around the numerous natural resources that wetlands offer. The skills that are needed to live from wetland resources are passed down through families for many generations.

These people plan their farming and other food-gathering activities so that they can benefit from the wetlands' natural wet and dry cycles. People living in rural societies that depend on wetland resources know how to use farming methods that utilize all the natural attributes of wetlands. They know from past experience which crops do well in wetland environments and when to plant and harvest these crops according to the wetlands' annual wet and dry periods. They know when they can expect to have success with fishing and when they will have the best opportunity to hunt the animals that come to wetlands in search of food and water.

A village built on a marsh in Iraq. This community depends upon the unusual characteristics of wetlands, including the wetlands' characteristic wet-dry cycle, which allows certain crops to thrive.

In a collection of writings called *Wetlands*, tropical ecology expert Patrick Denny writes: "The lives of people in many rural economies are geared to, and revolve around, the functioning of wetlands. At the individual family, village, and community level, the wetland is there to serve their needs."

Wetland tribes

The floodplain wetlands along rivers such as the Nile in Africa are home to many tribal cultures. Among these are the Nilotic peoples, who live in the sudd, or swampy, region of Sudan, a nation in northern Africa. Nearly four hundred thousand people belong to three Nilotic tribes—Dinka, Nuer, and Shilluk—that live there. They all use wetland resources in some way to obtain food and other items needed for daily life. The Dinka and Nuer tribes raise cattle and use the floodplain grasslands along the White Nile River, a tributary of the Nile, for cattle grazing. The Shilluk tribe also raises cattle, but they depend mostly on the crops grown in the floodplain wetland during the wet season. All three tribes fish and raise crops such as maize, beans, and sorghum. Their farming, grazing, and fishing activities are planned around the annual flooding of the White Nile River and the moisture that the floodwaters supply to the grasslands in the river's floodplain.

Materials obtained from wetlands provide for other needs, as well. The homes of many wetland tribes are built from the plant materials found in the wetlands. Tropical ecologist Patrick Denny writes:

> In an African village abutting a wetland, the elegantly reed-thatched houses and huts might well, for example, be constructed from wetland materials—be they timbers from mangroves, trunks from

palm trees and bundles of papyrus. The walls might be of brick or clay and muds from the wetland sediments; the floors might be strewn with dried cattail and Myrtle for sweet aromas or with mats woven from reeds, raphia [raffia] palm leaflets or papyrus.

The benefits of wetlands are not limited to Third World communities. Farmers and ranchers in developed countries benefit from wetlands in their fields, although not all farmers and ranchers understand or appreciate the benefits. Many types of wetland plants can be used as food for livestock. Marsh grasses, rushes, sedges, reeds, canary grass, and other wild grasses that grow in abundance in wetland areas make excellent food for cattle. Domestic hay also grows well in and around many wetland areas. W. Alan Wentz, of the South Dakota Cooperative Wildlife Research Unit, says:

> In many parts of the U.S. farmers have grown to depend on the hay crops that wetlands can provide annually. In drought years the wetland basin may be the only part of the farm that produces a harvestable crop. And in normal years a farmer can almost always take a hay crop from the edge of a wetland as natural drying occurs during the summer.

A farmer bales salt marsh hay in Newburyport, Massachusetts. Many wetland grasses can be used for feeding livestock.

People who live in urban settings in the industrialized world also depend on the resources wetlands offer. But since most people in the developed world do not go directly to the wetlands for food, water, or other materials, they often do not realize how many wetland resources they actually use.

Seafood is one important product of wetlands. The rich mix of fish and shellfish that live near or spawn in wetlands provide an important source of food for humans. The slightly salty marshes found along coastal bays and the mouths of rivers are among the most productive ecosystems on earth. This is because the tides are constantly delivering rich nutrients into these estuarine marshes, which are water passages where the ocean tide meets a river current. G. Tyler Miller Jr., author of *Living in the Environment*, says:

> This high productivity occurs because the tidelands are nutrient sinks. They trap rich silt and organic matter that rivers wash down from the land, and then hold and use these nutrients to produce an extraordinary bloom of life. The plants (mostly grasses) growing in estuaries, swamps and marshes are not very useful for human consumption, but these areas are very important as food sources, homes, and spawning grounds for many types of

Shrimp boats lie within a wetland marsh. Wetlands offer incredibly rich soil, which fosters plant and animal life. Tons of fish and shellfish are harvested from such areas each year.

shellfish and commercial and sport saltwater fish
that are a vital source of protein for humans.

Fish and shellfish harvested from coastal wetlands produce tons of food for human consump-
tion annually. In the United States over $10 bil-
lion worth of wetland-dependent fish and shellfish are harvested every year. They include
salmon, flounder, bass and bluefish, clams, oys-
ters, crabs, shrimp, and lobsters.

Protection from floods and storms

Wetlands also benefit humans by providing
flood control. They are natural water storage systems. Many wetland plants have the ability to
hold and store water in their roots, leaves, and
stems. Sedge, a grasslike plant that commonly
grows in wetlands, can store large amounts of
water in its leaves and roots, for example. The
soil found in wetlands also helps to prevent
floods. Wetland soil is porous, meaning that it has
the ability to hold more water than dryland soils.
Even small wetland areas can hold back large
amounts of water. For example, a ten-acre marsh
can store over 1.5 million gallons of floodwater.
Wetland plants that grow in the floodplains along
rivers and streams prevent the soil from eroding
during floods. This is because the root systems of
wetland plants bind particles of soil together and
keep them from being swept away when the water level is high.

It is normal for rivers and streams to flood oc-
casionally. This is not usually a concern for
homes, farms, and other commercial develop-
ments built outside of the floodplain. But because
of the attraction of building close to water, many
homes, businesses, and farms have been built
within floodplains. To protect people and their
property, structures such as dams, levees, berms,
dikes, and floodgates have been built to hold back

Although dams prevent severe flooding, they destroy wetland areas.

and control the water. Often these structures destroy marshes, swamps, and other types of floodplain wetlands in the process.

While flood-control structures usually work, they cannot be counted on all the time. Extremely strong rains and swift currents can render them useless or destroy them. In the summer of 1993 people living near the Mississippi River in the American Midwest experienced an extremely severe flood. It was one of the worst floods in North America in this century. It killed at least fifty people, left seventy thousand homeless, and caused nearly $12 billion in property damage. Portions of nine states—North Dakota, Iowa, Illinois, Kansas, Minnesota, Mississippi, Wisconsin, South Dakota, and Nebraska—suffered so much damage that they were classified as federal disaster areas.

River control backfires

Many experts believe that the severity of the Mississippi River's flooding was partly due to the destruction of wetlands and attempts to artificially control the flow of the river by means of dams, levees, and other such structures. Nature writer William Stolzenburg says:

> Ecologists concluded that the myriad . . . dams, levees and straightenings aimed at shackling the Mississippi have backfired, restraining the beneficial floods and inviting the catastrophic ones. Eighty percent of the wetlands that once soaked up the flood waters have been plowed or paved. The flood has people rethinking the wisdom of strong-arming the Mississippi.

Environmental organizations are using this flood to remind the general public about the value of preserving wetlands as a means of flood protection. They hope that by studying the flood of 1993, scientists, environmentalists, and engineers can learn much about the role wetlands play in flood control. They believe that instead of creating tighter channels of flood walls, levees, and dams to contain the river, flooding could be better prevented by restoring as many floodplain wetlands as possible. Kevin Coyle, president of the environmental group American Rivers, is a leading proponent of this idea. He says:

National Guardsmen and volunteers repair a break in a sandbag levee that is protecting houses during a 1993 flood in Genevieve, Missouri. Scientists are just now beginning to understand the role wetlands play in preventing such floods.

Reprinted by permission of Chuck Asay and Creators Syndicate.

The flood of 1993 gives us the opportunity to learn about rivers and their natural forces. We can now begin to turn around our longstanding efforts to control nature and restore rivers to their natural floodplains by creating wetlands and buffer zones along the river.

Natural flood control

The Charles River, located in eastern Massachusetts near the city of Boston, is a good example of how wetlands can be used for flood control. The U.S. Army Corps of Engineers purchased the wetland areas north of the Charles River so that they could be preserved as a means of natural flood control. They did this after they determined that the 8,422 acres of wetlands north of the river provided the most cost-effective way of controlling the Charles River and minimizing flood damage. When floodwaters rise, the wetlands north of the Charles River are able to absorb much of the water. This protects Boston and the other cities and towns downstream by decreasing the height and the speed of the river's flow.

While some downstream flooding occurs along the Charles River from time to time, it is not as severe as it would have been without the wetlands' protection. The Corps of Engineers determined that if the wetlands were filled and flood-control structures built, the annual cost of floodwater damage could rise as much as $17 million per year. The U.S. Environmental Protection Agency publication *Beyond the Estuary* states:

> The Charles River Basin still remains a prime example of controlling flooding using the natural process of . . . wetlands. This method was found to be not only the most effective means of flood control, but also the most economical.

A buffer against storms

Coastal wetlands also protect nearby communities. They lessen the impact of storm damage by acting as a buffer when water from coastal storms, such as hurricanes and typhoons, pushes inland. The trees and other plants that grow in wetlands absorb much of the storm's rain and wind. Wetland plants are able to withstand these storms much better than structures such as homes and other buildings. The tragic storms and flooding in Bangladesh are an example of what can happen when coastal wetlands are destroyed. For several decades the mangrove trees along Bangladesh's coast on the Bay of Bengal have gradually been removed so that more land could be used for farming. Once they were cleared, these coastal wetlands were used to raise the extra rice needed to feed the country's growing population.

Rice crops grow well in the moist, soggy soil that once supported a mangrove swamp. On the delta of Bangladesh's Bay of Bengal alone, nearly fifty-five thousand square miles of wetlands have been converted to farmland.

The additional rice supply helped feed more of the nation's people, but a high price was ultimately paid for creating this additional farmland. When the mangrove trees were removed, so was the bay's protection from floods and storms. As recently as 1990, typhoons hit Bangladesh, killing over 131,000 people and making millions homeless. Damages were estimated to be over $2.7 billion. The conditions left by the storm in this already impoverished country caused disease to spread rapidly through the population. In areas where the mangrove wetlands still exist, storm damage is usually much less severe than in areas where the trees have been removed.

Pollution filters

If wetlands are not overtaxed with waste, they act as pollution filter systems for groundwater, rivers, streams, and lakes. The roots of wetland plants, and eventually the plants themselves, are

Although the destruction wreaked by this 1991 cyclone in Bangladesh could not have been completely eliminated, scientists believe that such damage can be minimized when communities leave their wetlands intact.

Water hyacinths are useful in absorbing pollutants in wetland areas. Many plants that thrive in wetland areas have similar properties.

able to trap and hold pollutants in the soggy mud. As long as the pollution is not too toxic, or poisonous, for the plants to endure, the wetland will continue to purify the water that flows through it. Water hyacinths, for example, which grow in warm climates, are especially good at trapping and absorbing nitrogen and phosphorus, chemicals that are commonly used in fertilizers and transported to wetlands by the runoff from farms.

Because wetlands are so effective at filtering pollutants, some mining and paper mill companies, along with companies in other industries, have constructed artificial wetlands to help purify water. Artificial wetlands are also being used to purify water from some residential areas. In the United States, over two hundred artificial wetlands have been constructed to process wastewater, or sewage. Creating artificial wetlands for this purpose is often less expensive than building a water-treatment plant to do the same job. Helen J. Challand, a professor of science education at National-Louis University, in Evanston, Illinois, says:

> Two acres of wetlands can do as good a job of purifying water as a $150,000 sewage-disposal plant,

perhaps even better because the sand and gravel used in the [disposal] plant aren't very effective filters. The muddy bottom of a wetland can really trap pollutants and keep them from entering the groundwater.

Arcata, California, located 280 miles north of San Francisco, is one town that uses artificial wetlands to purify its sewer water. In the early 1980s town officials were told that Arcata's sewer water did not meet quality standards. When local officials found out how expensive it would be to build a water-treatment plant, they opted to create artificial wetlands instead. They transformed an abandoned county dump and the remains of a lumber mill into ninety-six acres of artificial wetlands. The cost of the project was about $676,000—far less than what a sewage-treatment plant would have cost. The water that now flows into Humboldt Bay from Arcata is cleaner than water discharged from a traditional sewage-treatment plant.

In addition to purifying water, wetlands also serve as a natural reservoir for underground water supplies. When the underground water supply dries up during a drought, water from nearby wetlands drains down to lower layers of rock and soil, restoring the water supply. Sometimes large wetlands act as a reservoir for communities miles away. Dr. Jay D. Hair, president of the National Wildlife Federation says:

> It has been calculated that the Lawrence Swamp, a 2,700-acre wetland in Massachusetts, recharges the shallow aquifer [water-bearing layer of sand, gravel, or rock] below it at the rate of eight million gallons per day. The wetland recharges an area of 16 square miles, and provides much of the water supply for Amherst, Massachusetts.

Recreational uses

Wetlands also serve the human need for recreation. Nature study, waterfowl hunting, hiking,

Artificial wetlands in Arcata, California, purify the town's sewer water by trapping and holding pollutants.

fishing, and boating are only some of the wetland-related recreational pursuits that are popular throughout the world. The U.S. Fish and Wildlife Service estimates that approximately fifty-five million people in the United States alone enjoy observing and photographing birds and other wetland-dependent wildlife as a recreational activity. Hunters in the United States spend over $300 million a year hunting wetland-dependent waterfowl. Some of the funds that are generated by these wetland-related activities are used to help preserve or restore wetlands. For example, the Federal Duck Stamp, which every waterfowl hunter is required by law to purchase along with a hunting license, is a major source of funding for waterfowl habitat protection. The funds generated by wetland-related recreational activities are equally important in other countries. Kai Curry-Lindahl, author of *Conservation for Survival—An Ecological Strategy* says:

A couple sets up equipment outside a marsh to bird-watch. Hunters also use wetlands to hunt ducks and geese.

> For many areas in different parts of the world, the recreational activities on or about lakes and marshes are the chief source of income. The recreational utilization of a wetland is often in direct proportion to its importance as a waterfowl habitat.

Many people are just beginning to realize the importance of wetlands. But at the same time, wetlands around the world are being destroyed at an alarming rate. If society is to continue to enjoy the many benefits wetlands offer to humanity, more must be done to prevent their destruction.

4

A Threatened Resource

WETLANDS AROUND THE WORLD are being threatened for many different reasons. Farming, urban development, industry, water projects, oil drilling, chemical pollution, harvesting peat, and the introduction of foreign weeds and plants have caused many wetlands around the world to be damaged or destroyed.

Farming is probably the single greatest cause of wetland destruction worldwide, followed by urban development. This pattern can clearly be seen in the United States, where decades of government policies and programs encouraged agricultural and urban development at the expense of wetlands. A twenty-year study by the U.S. Fish and Wildlife Service revealed that an average of 458,000 acres of wetlands were destroyed in the United States every year between the 1950s and 1970s. This figure was determined by comparing aerial photographs of wetland areas taken in the early 1950s to those taken in the mid-1970s. During the twenty years covered by the survey, researchers discovered that 6 million acres of forested wetlands, 400,000 acres of shrub swamp, 4.7 million acres of inland marshes, and 400,000

(Opposite page) A marsh sits outside the towering city landscape of Portland, Oregon. Many wetlands are endangered by urban encroachment.

Ducks thrive in the waters of Horicon Marsh, Wisconsin, in August 1900.

acres of coastal marshes were destroyed. Agricultural use accounted for 87 percent of this loss.

Farmers drain and fill

Part of the reason for the rapid pace of wetland destruction can be found in U.S. policies and programs in place during much of that time. Until the middle of this century the U.S. government actively encouraged people to drain wetlands and convert them to farmlands. The government backed up its position by making technical and financial assistance available to those who needed it. This process began in the mid-1800s when Congress passed the Swamp Land Acts of 1849, 1850, and 1860. These acts gave sixty-five million acres of federally controlled wetlands to the states to be used for farming, industry, and housing. About a hundred years later, in 1940, the U.S. Department of Agriculture formed the Agricultural Conservation Program. This program provided technical and financial assistance to farmers who wished to drain wetlands on their property. Many farmers considered wetlands in their fields to be wasted space. Once filled, however, a wetland could be put to use for raising crops, along with the rest of the fields. This proved to be a quick and inexpensive method of obtaining more usable land. During the forty years this program was in effect, fifty-seven million acres of wetlands disappeared in the United States.

The draining and filling of wetlands for farming needs has occurred all across North America. One type of wetland that farmers routinely drained and filled to make room for crops were prairie potholes. Prairie potholes are important to waterfowl. They are used as nesting sites for ducks and geese. So when prairie pothole wetlands are destroyed, nesting sites for waterfowl are limited. This forces the birds to crowd into the few wetlands that are available or make their nests in inadequately small wetland areas that can only partially serve their needs. When large flocks of ducks crowd into small areas, they use up food more quickly and are more vulnerable to being killed by predators and hunters. The crowding of ducks and other waterfowl also increases the spread of diseases such as avian cholera, which killed nearly a hundred thousand waterfowl in Nebraska's Rainwater Basin area during the spring of 1980.

Upsetting the balance

The commercial farming methods of the developed world now being used in many developing nations have added to loss of wetlands around the world. Western farming methods use imported hybrid or mixed-variety seed, artificial irrigation systems, chemical fertilizers and pesticides, and machinery that can only be operated on flat, dry land. Native seed and crop varieties often grow within or near wetlands. But farmers who use imported hybrid seed often must take extra measures to insure that it will grow. Many hybrid seed varieties, which are developed by cross-breeding existing varieties of plants, were

Horicon Marsh is dredged in 1914 (left), and becomes a productive field soon after drainage (right). In their efforts to create arable land, the federal government destroyed acres of wetlands and destroyed wildlife habitat along with it.

originally developed in cooler climates and are not as vigorous or disease resistant when they are planted in semitropical or tropical locations. They often require large amounts of pesticides, fungicides, fertilizers, and irrigation systems in order to grow. When agricultural chemicals reach wetlands, they upset the chemical balance of the ecosystem, causing some plants to die and others to grow more quickly than they should. These chemicals are also harmful to many of the animals that live in the wetland. Irrigation systems harm wetlands because they redirect water that would otherwise flow into wetlands.

Wetland destruction for agriculture

Third World governments, wanting to produce more food for both local use and export, often encourage the destruction of wetlands for commercial farming. In *Wetlands*, tropical ecology expert Patrick Denny writes:

> In Africa, colonial governments and subsequent aid programs have instigated [urged] the drainage and clearance of wetlands for food production. There is no doubt that wetland clearance for agriculture has been highly successful. But the trade-off is habitat loss and degradation of the environment.

The need for food and income weighs heavily on the governments of developing nations. Often these needs take priority over preserving wetland ecosystems. Since the 1950s, for example, many valley swamps in Rwanda and Uganda have been drained for farming purposes, according to *Wetlands in Danger: A World Conservation Atlas*. Edward Maltby, of the University of Exeter's geography department in Great Britain explains.

> The pressures are immense on developing countries to increase basic food production, reduce waterborne diseases and attempt to raise living standards. Even if the long term benefits of retaining those wetland resources can be demonstrated, the

Once a thriving wetland area, this section of Southeast China has been destroyed by over-farming.

"ON SECOND THOUGHT, MAYBE WE SHOULD CONSIDER JUST STAYING SOUTH THIS WINTER!"

social and economic problems facing the Third World nations are immediate and urgent.

Urban development—and all of the services required for serving urban communities—have displaced wetlands in many regions of the world. Wetlands have been drained and filled to make room for factories, houses, hotels, shopping malls, marinas, and golf courses. Draining and filling in of wetlands has been especially attractive to developers in areas where land costs are high. Approximately 13 percent of the wetland loss in the United States between 1950 and 1970 resulted from residential and commercial land development. A 1987 National Wildlife Federation report states:

> Wetlands [in urban settings] are destroyed by filling areas for home sites, constructing highways,

A boardwalk across the wetlands allows beach access from this hotel in Florida. Until very recently, construction took precedence over preserving delicate wetland habitat.

[draining] for mosquito control, dredging canals and waterways, disposing of dredging materials, and constructing industrial and commercial complexes in or adjacent to wetlands.

This problem is most severe along the nation's coastal wetland areas, especially in the states of California, Florida, New York, New Jersey, and Texas. In southern Florida, for example, hundreds of thousands of acres of mangrove swamps were destroyed between 1950 and 1970 to make room for hotels, condominiums, houses, resorts, and marinas.

Water projects

Governments in many countries have built dams, levees, and other structures to control and redirect the flow of rivers and streams for urban or agricultural use, to prevent flooding, and to provide hydroelectric power to nearby communities. Though probably unintended, many wetlands have been destroyed by these types of projects. When water is rerouted from its natural path, tributaries dry up. When tributaries no longer flow, wetlands fed by those tributaries also dry up. At the very least, a wetland that loses its source of water will develop an imbalance in its carefully balanced ecosystem.

The Everglades wetlands, located in southern Florida, have been severely damaged by government water projects. The natural path of the 103-mile-long Kissimmee River was altered in the 1960s, and nearly fifty thousand acres of nearby wetlands were destroyed. This destruction took place when the U.S. Army Corps of Engineers built a fifty-six-mile-long and thirty-foot-deep canal to control the river's path. The project was intended to control flooding and provide more water for farmers, real estate developers, and other commercial concerns. The extra water supply was needed to handle the needs of the state's increasing population.

Many sections of the Everglades dried out after the river's path had been altered. The lack of water has killed many wetland plants and forced out or killed many wetland animals and birds. Nature writer William Stolzenburg describes the changes in the Everglades:

> Within the last century, 1,400 miles of machine-dug canals have siphoned the sprawling river in foreign directions. This artificial plumbing has drained thousands of square miles of wetlands to create farmlands and other areas. The Everglades—the famous river of grass through which much of this water once flowed—has shrunk to half of its original four million acres.

Wetlands in other parts of the world have also suffered from water projects, most of which were intended to improve daily life for local human inhabitants. While the continent of Africa still has many of its natural wetlands, many are now being threatened. Dams are being built to produce hydroelectric power for farms, urban areas, and heavy industry. These projects are bringing power to regions of Africa that need a dependable supply of electricity in order to modernize and attract new industry.

The Florida Everglades provide homes for many different bird species, including these egrets and ibises.

In an attempt to control flooding, the U.S. Army Corps of Engineers diverted the flow of Florida's Kissimmee River. Acres of wetlands were destroyed when the newly diverted river stopped feeding water to these areas.

But to produce this hydroelectric power, dams are built that stop or slow the natural flooding of rivers. This causes floodplain wetland ecosystems to dry up, making it impossible to support wetland-dependent plants and animals. One such project in Zambia, in south central Africa, has ruined five million acres of floodplain wetlands. The Zambian government built two dams on the Kafue River to power hydroelectric plants. The project caused the entire wetland floodplain on the western side of the Kafue River to dry up. Wildlife in the Kafue Flats floodplain, adapted to the alternating yearly cycles of mud and floods, could no longer thrive in the new environment.

Chemical pollution

The effects of chemical pollutants on wetlands are sometimes hard to measure, but researchers believe that urban, industrial, and agricultural pollutants have harmed wetlands. Most of the damaging chemical pollutants are not dumped directly into wetlands. They may have been disposed of in an area that drains into a wetland such as a river or stream, or they may have been carried into feeder rivers and streams by rainwater. Pollutants that enter wetlands in this way are known as nonpoint pollution. Nonpoint pollution does not come from a single source. It can be anything from oil that leaks from cars and trucks to spilled or carelessly disposed-of products from residences, businesses, and industry.

Chemicals that are commonly used in agriculture can also find their way into wetlands. Runoff—pesticides and other chemicals that run off farmland—can poison wetlands. The United States alone uses about four hundred thousand tons of pesticides every year. Only about 1 percent of the pesticides used actually kills the pests for which they were intended. The rest of the pes-

Human ignorance has allowed hazardous waste to destroy many wetland areas with pollutants. Unfortunately, a major source of groundwater is also destroyed in the process.

ticides filter into the air, soil, or water. Even fertilizer runoff from gardens and farms can damage wetlands because it upsets the ecosystem's natural chemical balance. The amount of fertilizer that gets into wetlands and other related water supplies is on the increase. In 1950, 14 million tons of fertilizer was used in the United States. By 1990, 140 million tons of fertilizer was used by farmers and gardeners. Nearly half of all fertilizer eventually runs off into nearby water supplies, and some of it flows into wetland areas. Most fertilizer contains nitrogen and phosphorus. When these chemicals enter wetland ecosystems, they cause algae and other aquatic plants to grow too quickly and overpopulate wetlands. This crowds out other wetland plants and causes them to weaken or die.

Wastes from industries such as chemical factories, oil refineries, paper mills, metal foundries, mines, and other heavy industries contain copper, lead, cyanide, mercury, dioxin, zinc, and other hazardous substances that are dangerous to plants and animals. Many industries have been permitted to dump these hazardous materials directly into wetlands. General Electric Company in Pittsfield, Massachusetts, drained waste products, including cancer-causing PCB (polychlorinated biphenyls), into a nearby river. When the river flooded, the harmful chemicals were carried onto the river's floodplain wetland and into nearby ponds. The company continued to flush its chemical waste into the river until the federal government halted the practice in 1977.

A textile mill on Saco River in Bideford, Maine. Many industries purposely built alongside wetlands in order to have a convenient place to dump such waste.

Oil and gas drilling

Oil and gas drilling operations, both inland and offshore, pose a hazard to nearby wetland ecosystems also. Accidental spills and movement of heavy equipment endangers the wetlands' deli-

Offshore oil drilling threatens wetland environments when accidental leaks or spills make their way ashore.

Workers attempt a Sisyphian task as they sponge up the oil from the Exxon Valdez *disaster in 1989. The spill wreaked havoc on nearby wetlands.*

cate environmental balance. Spills that result from offshore oil drilling can severely damage a wetland. When oil is spilled in offshore drilling operations, much of it is carried by tides into coastal swamps and marshes. In 1989 when the *Exxon Valdez* ran aground on the Bligh Reef in the Prince William Sound off the southern coast of Alaska, it spilled over ten million gallons of oil. Much of this oil washed ashore, contaminating Alaska's southern coastal wetlands. Oil from the spill killed many shorebirds, sea mammals, fish, and other animals. Many wetland plants were also killed or weakened as a result of the spill.

Wetlands along Alaska's Pacific coast are also in danger of being damaged by oil and gas drilling operations. In order for oil and gas companies to reach their fields, many pieces of heavy machinery must be brought in. Pipes must be laid to transport the fuel. The movement of the heavy vehicles and machines necessary for these operations over the frail, semifrozen surface of the Alaskan tundra wetlands creates deep ruts, which allow salty seawater to enter freshwater wetlands. This saltwater kills many freshwater animals and plants, destroying the natural ecosystem.

The building of the Alaskan pipeline destroyed many wetland areas when crews and machinery were brought in over the delicate soil.

Marshes in Louisiana have been damaged in much the same way as the Alaskan tundra wetlands. The inflow of saltwater through access canals and the equipment tracks left by drilling operations have killed many freshwater marsh plants that are not able to survive in a saltwater environment. In an article for *Audubon* magazine, nature writer Donald G. Schueler says:

> Thousands of access canals and pipelines have cut Louisiana's coastal plain to ribbons, inviting saltwater intrusion and aborting the natural overflow pattern of the marsh. In a mere handful of years, erosion and saltwater intrusion have destroyed tens of thousands of marsh acres adjoining the channels.

Imported plants

While some wetland ecosystems have been damaged by the inflow of saltwater, others have been harmed by the introduction of weeds and other plants that are foreign to the area. Imported plants and weeds, which are intentionally or accidentally transported from one part of the world to another, are sometimes much more vigorous than those that are native to the wetland environment.

When new kinds of plants crowd out plants that are native to the area, the natural ecosystem changes. Since many native wetland plants grow only in specific kinds of wetland areas, the introduction of new, more vigorous, imported plants can put them in danger of extinction.

The purple loosestrife, an herb nicknamed the beautiful killer by the Canadian Wildlife Federation, is one example. During the 1800s purple loosestrife seeds were accidentally transported by ship from Europe to North America. The plant has now spread throughout much of the eastern and midwestern sections of the United States and Canada. Purple loosestrife is a tall, flowering plant that can produce thousands of seeds during a growing season. It can quickly take over a wetland area, crowding out many native wetland plant species.

Purple loosestrife is another example of a nonnative plant dominating delicate wetland ecosystems. Incredibly productive, loosestrife has choked out many other native plant species.

The introduction of such plants can cause drastic changes in the original wetland ecosystem, making it impossible for many native wetland plants and animals to obtain the food they need to survive there. Only recently has the seriousness of this problem come to light. Don Schmitz, a biologist with Florida's Department of Natural Resources, is working to bring this problem to national attention. In an interview in the January/February 1994 issue of *Sierra* magazine, Schmitz says, "In the last ten years, we've probably lost more habitat to exotic plant species than to development."

Removing these invading plants is the only known way to stop their spread. But the process is time consuming and expensive. When Everglades National Park officials decided to remove sixty acres of invading Brazilian peppertrees, it cost over $16,000 an acre to bulldoze them out. It will cost around $100 million to rehabilitate an additional four thousand acres of the Everglades National Park that has been taken over by the Brazilian peppertree. The tremendous expense involved in removing these invading plants severely limits the number of such projects that can be taken on in the near future.

Peat bogs

Another way wetlands are damaged is by harvesting too many of their products. This is especially true of the harvest of peat from bogs. Peat, which is composed of layers of dead, compressed moss, is sold to nurseries, gardeners, and farmers. Peat is useful for agriculture because it holds

Thousands of dollars have been spent by Everglades park officials to control the Brazilian peppertree.

large amounts of water, providing moisture for plants during dry periods. Peat is also dried and burned as fuel or to produce electricity in some parts of the world.

Most of the world's peat bogs are located in the Northern Hemisphere. Half of the peat bogs in the world are located in the former Soviet Union where more than seventy power plants burn peat for electricity. Canada, the world's second largest peat source, has been harvesting peat for agricultural and fuel use for over fifty years and has about 270 million acres of peatland. Canadians harvest nearly 40,000 acres of peat a year and export about 90 percent of it to the United States. In the United States, Florida and Minnesota have the largest areas of peat bogs.

Overharvesting

Most peat harvesters say that they are doing no permanent damage to bogs. However, it takes at least twenty-five years for bog plants to return to their previous state. Even then, only about 90 percent of the original flora, or plant life, will grow

Peat is cut for use in agriculture. In some areas, peat is overharvested, permanently changing the wetland environment.

Sphagnum moss is a mainstay of bogs. Dead and decaying moss forms peat and keeps bog soil absorbent and fertile.

back. If they are overharvested, peat bog ecosystems are among the most difficult types of wetlands to restore. This is because peat, which is made of decayed sphagnum moss and other plants, forms slowly. The process of decay and compression takes time. Several inches of peat may take a hundred years to form. This has prompted environmentalists in some countries to recommend a boycott of horticultural peat moss. In the May/ June 1993 issue of *Sierra*, nature writer Marc Lecard wrote:

> The mat of dead and living sphagnum literally supports the plant life of the bog. If sphagnum moss is not cut out completely, it will slowly grow back. But since it is the keystone of bog ecosystems, cutting it results in the destruction of many other plants as well as wildlife habitat.

As more wetlands are destroyed, it becomes increasingly difficult for wetland-dependent animals and plants to survive. This problem is especially serious for species that are already near extinction. This is why it is so important for the wetland ecosystems that remain to be preserved.

5

Restoring Wetlands

A DAMAGED WETLAND cannot provide suitable habitat for the plants and animals that depend on it for survival. As more wetlands are damaged or destroyed, wetland-dependent species find it more difficult to survive. Because wetlands are vital to the survival of many plants and animals, and because of their importance to human communities as well, scientists and others are attempting to restore dying wetland habitats. Through restoration, damaged wetlands can be, at least to some degree, returned to their former state.

Growing interest in this new field of scientific and conservation work has spawned an organization devoted to restoration of wetlands and other types of damaged ecosystems. The Society for Ecological Restoration was established in 1989 to help conservation scientists exchange information and ideas that may advance their restoration work. The society presently has over twenty-two hundred members.

(Opposite page) Members of the Army Corps of Engineers attempt a wetland restoration by laying willow wattles and brush matting.

Problems with restoring wetlands

Restoring a wetland involves much more than just replacing the water or planting a few plants. Scientists must determine exactly what kind of

67

damage has occurred to the wetland and how severe the problem is before anything can be done to restore it. Once restoration starts, success is by no means guaranteed. Like most of earth's natural formations, wetlands developed over thousands, and in some cases millions, of years. Some, like prairie potholes, developed under conditions created millions of years ago. Because researchers cannot duplicate those conditions, their challenge is in restoring the end result. This work requires knowledge, care, and patience. Susan M. Galatowitsch, a botanist at the University of Minnesota in Minneapolis, says:

California is one state with a large amount of wetland destruction. Here a man measures plant growth as part of a restoration project in California.

> There is a widely held belief that prairie potholes,
> many of which were drained for agricultural pur-
> poses, are easy to restore: just return the water.
> But the ecosystems of these ponds, originally cre-
> ated by the surging of glaciers, may not be so
> amenable [obedient] to quick rehabilitation.

The longer a wetland has been dry, the more difficult it is to restore. A wetland that has been dry for a long period of time is unlikely to have original plants or seeds. Without these plants or seeds, a wetland cannot be restored. So ecologists must search for and collect starter plants and seeds from other similar wetlands. Although this can be done, it is a time-consuming process. In some instances so many acres of wetlands have been destroyed or damaged in a region that the necessary plants are difficult to find. Southern California, for example, has lost 75 percent of its coastal wetlands. California today has only 31,700 acres of coastal wetland habitat. This loss has caused 187 plant and 94 animal species that depend on the state's wetlands to become threatened or endangered. Joy B. Zedler, chief ecologist at the Pacific Estuarine Research Laboratory at San Diego State University, says, "California shows that if losses continue, you eventually get to a point where they cannot rebound if there is a catastrophic event. Species have to come back from somewhere, and there is not enough habitat left so they can recover."

Hard work and high expenses

Wetlands that have been dry for a long time present another problem. Weeds and other dry-land plants that have established themselves in the area since the wetland's destruction must all be removed before restoration work can begin. This too can be done, but it requires many hours of work. Other wetlands have been damaged by agricultural chemicals, oil, or other chemical toxins. These chemicals must first be removed before wetland plants and animals can be expected to survive there.

The costs of restoration vary from project to project, depending on size, the extent of restoration being attempted, and the level of expertise needed for the project's success. Marion Fishel, a marine ecologist with Shell Oil Company, has said:

> The costs for wetlands restoration are highly variable and have ranged from as little as $250 per acre for small and simple projects to many thousands of dollars per acre for more complex projects, such as the establishment of a marsh for sewage treatment.

Thousands of wetland restoration projects are being attempted by governments and ecology experts around the world. The government of Sweden, for example, plans to restore some of that nation's most vital wetland habitats. In one project the Swedish government plans to spend as much as $161 million to restore Lake Hornborga, a marsh in central Sweden that is important to many European waterbirds. The U.S. Fish and Wildlife Service has also taken an active role in wetland restoration efforts. In the past few decades the Fish and Wildlife Service has taken part in over a thousand wetland restoration projects.

Bringing back the Everglades

One of the largest wetland restoration projects ever attempted is the restoration of the Everglades National Park in southern Florida. A hundred years ago the Everglades covered four thousand square miles of land, stretching from Lake Okeechobee in the north to the southern tip of Florida. It was one hundred miles long, thirty miles wide at its narrowest point, and seventy-five miles

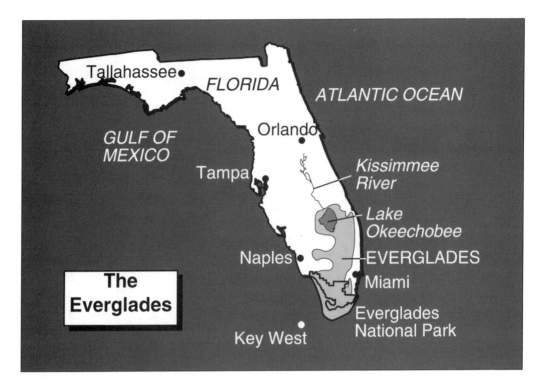

The Everglades

across at its widest point. The Everglades was vibrant and full of life. It was home to many kinds of fish, reptiles, amphibians, and mammals. It was home to large flocks of waterbirds that depended on the Everglades' abundant wetland resources for food, water, and nesting grounds.

The Everglades today is two-thirds of its original size. Within the last hundred years the Everglades has shrunk to twenty-seven hundred square miles. Its water supply has dwindled to one-fifth of what it once was. This change has caused a tremendous loss of wildlife habitat and made it difficult for many wetland-dependent animals and plants to survive. Only about 5 percent of the wading birds that nested in the Everglades a hundred years ago are still able to raise their young there. The loss of wetland habitat has pushed some birds, such as the wood stork, close to extinction. Jack Rudloe, author of *The Wilderness*

The Florida Everglades has vastly shrunk in size because it has been drained for agricultural purposes and for flood control. As a result, many species of animals have died, including fish, which this man attempts to find along the Kissimmee River in the Everglades.

Coast, writes: "The changes in water flow nearly destroyed the bird life and caused the rich fisheries in Florida Bay to collapse."

The damage

Damage to the Everglades started in the late 1800s, when land along the Kissimmee River and the wetland borders was drained to create more farm and ranch land. Little by little, as draining continued, the water level of the Everglades fell. Water projects in the 1960s further strained the natural balance in the Everglades. A federal project to redirect the Kissimmee River, one of the Everglades' main sources of water, made more water available to farmers and ranchers and for urban and commercial development. The project also aided with flood control. But the levees, canals, and dams required for these projects worsened the growing water shortage in the Everglades.

The combined effect of all these water projects has rerouted four-fifths of the water that would normally have flowed into the Everglades into cities, towns, and farms in other parts of the state. Archie Carr, author of *The Everglades*, writes:

> Although drought has always brought recurrent stress to the Everglades, nowadays the normal peril is increased by a growing water famine. Ever since the first canals were dug over a half-century ago . . . in order to drain water off the incredibly rich muckland soil . . . water levels in the Everglades have been falling. The dry seasons have become more pronounced, and catastrophic drought and the fires that follow occur more frequently.

The restoration of the Everglades began in 1993 and is expected to take at least twenty years to complete. The total cost promises to run into the hundreds of millions of dollars. No one has ever attempted a restoration project on this scale. Tom MacVicar, deputy executive director of the

An alligator hides within the thick vegetation of the Florida Everglades.

South Florida Water Management District, the state agency charged with the restoration, describes the magnitude of the project: "It's a daunting assignment for us. This is uncharted territory."

Challenges ahead

One of the biggest challenges in restoring the Everglades will be redirecting the Kissimmee River to its original path. Plans call for the river to be moved out of its containment channel and back into the winding natural route it once took. Once returned to that path, the river is expected to cover the floodplain and flow back into Lake Okeechobee, restoring habitat for more than three

Part of the Everglades restoration project would include restoring Kissimmee River to its original bed, which allowed it to flow to Lake Okeechobee (pictured). If completed, the Lake would experience a repopulation of plant and animal species.

hundred fish and wildlife species, including the endangered wood stork and snail kite.

The Corps of Engineers estimates that this part of the restoration project will cost at least $372 million and take ten to fifteen years to complete. Ike Flores, writer for the Associated Press, says:

> The plan is simply to fill in 22 miles of the canal and force the river to spill out onto the floodplain and find its own way to Okeechobee. Engineers expect the river will generally return to its old, meandering bed, which never was filled in. The work will result in restoring some 26,500 acres of wetlands and 40 square miles of river-and-floodplain ecosystem.

Filtering out chemicals

Another major challenge for those involved in the restoration efforts is the construction of forty thousand acres of artificial marshes that will serve as a protective buffer around the park. These marshes will be used to catch or filter out pesticides, fertilizers, and other farm runoff before they reach the Everglades. These chemicals must be filtered out because they upset the balance of the Everglades' plant life. William Booth, writer for the *Washington Post*, says:

> Phosphorus [in the Everglades] sets off a chain reaction, stimulating [heavy growth] among bacteria and algae, encouraging the growth of cattails that choke the marshes. Thousands of acres have been taken over by cattails in the past decade in the Loxahatchee refuge and water conservation areas to the north of Everglades National Park.

The federal government estimates that marsh construction will cost at least $700 million. Farmers are expected to pay up to $332 million of that cost, with federal, state, and local governments providing the rest.

If the first forty thousand acres of artificial marshes are not found to be doing an adequate

Cattails can thrive in water that has a high level of pollutants, choking out more fragile plantlife.

job by the year 2002, an additional thirty-six thousand acres of farmland near the Everglades will be purchased and turned into artificial marshes. All of this must be done before the Everglades can once again be a fully functioning wetland ecosystem.

A mixed record of success

Artificial wetlands have a mixed record of success. When properly constructed, they have demonstrated at least some of the benefits of natural wetlands. Some of the basic functions, such as establishing plants that purify water by trapping chemicals and other impurities, are relatively simple to achieve. Helen J. Challand, professor of science education at National-Louis University, has said: "Those functions we can duplicate somewhat include improving water quality, storing flood waters and releasing them slowly and trapping sediments."

But creating artificial wetlands that are designed to totally replace the ecological functions of natural wetlands is a much more difficult task. A slight difference in the type of soil that is used in an artificial wetland, for example, could prevent some types of wetland plants from growing. And the absence of those plants might make it impossible for some wetland-dependent animals to find the food they need. According to Marguerite Holloway, author of an article in the April 1994 issue of *Scientific American:*

> If scientists want to return an environment to its "natural" state, they need a full understanding of what that is, how the particular ecology is constantly changing and how human beings fit into it. No one has, or is likely to have such insight.

Even when designers of artificial wetlands succeed at duplicating many of the ecological functions of a natural wetland, it takes time for the birds and other animals that depend on wetland ecosystems to find this new wetland and make it their home. It also takes time to make sure that the wetland will continue to function as the kind of ecosystem it was created to be. Marion Fishel of Shell Oil Company has said: "A newly created wetland is especially vulnerable to disturbances, and it takes a considerable period of time to be certain that such a wetland has been successfully established."

More research is needed

Joy Zedler of San Diego State University favors research on the creation of artificial wetlands but does not believe that the science has advanced enough to permit them to adequately replace existing wetlands. Since 1987 she has been monitoring the Sweetwater Marsh near San Diego, California, that was created to compensate for wetlands that had been destroyed during the construction of a nearby highway. The wetland was designed primarily as a habitat for light-footed clapper rails, an endangered species of waterbird. Even though the salt marsh was designed especially to meet the needs of these endangered birds, no light-footed clapper rails have occupied the marsh since its construction. Zedler says:

> I don't think we are ever going to get functional equivalency for the marsh. It's hard to create wetlands because we don't know what all of nature's building materials were. They're made up of thousands of species and [underlying layers] that are compatible with a region's [water characteristics] and climate. There are millions of pieces in an ecosystem, and we have only looked at a tiny fraction of them. Some are still undiscovered. It is not as easy to restore these systems as developers would have us think. If we allow all our natural wetlands to be replaced by man-made ones, I guarantee you that we will lose biodiversity.

There is still much controversy over artificial wetlands' effectiveness as a satisfactory substitute for the wetlands that are being destroyed by agriculture and commercial development. While artificial wetlands might look like wetlands and

Surrounded by the artificial Sweetwater Marsh in San Diego, California, Joy Zedler conducts ongoing research to see whether such marshes can effectively replace their destroyed counterparts.

Sweetwater Marsh in San Diego was originally constructed to provide a home for the light-footed clapper rail, whose habitat was being destroyed at an alarming rate. Unfortunately, the clapper rail has never taken up residence in the marsh.

duplicate many functions of wetlands, they might not serve as satisfactory habitat for many animals and plants. Even under the best conditions it usually takes at least several years for an artificial wetland to come close to taking the place of a natural wetland ecosystem.

More to learn

The science of creating wetlands is still in its infancy. Much more must be learned before scientists can truly understand what is necessary to make an artificial wetland succeed. William E. Odem, an environmentalist at the University of Virginia, says:

> Created wetlands offer an exciting opportunity through monitoring and study to better understand natural processes of wetlands development. Unfortunately, there are very few projects which have been followed for more than several years after their completion. If we can implement long-term monitoring of created wetland sites, it may be possible in the future to not only predict artificial wetland development with better precision, but also to better understand the natural process of wetlands development and change.

6

Protecting Wetlands

ONE OF THE MOST important steps in preserving wetlands is giving them government protection. Governments can best protect wetlands by establishing clear goals and policies and by passing laws that penalize those who damage or destroy wetlands. In the past few decades governments around the world have become increasingly concerned about protecting wetland resources. As a result of this concern, many nations have passed laws that are helping to protect these vital resources from destruction.

Early wetland conservation efforts

People first became concerned about protecting wetlands because of their importance as waterfowl habitats. When conservationists and hunters noticed a drop in waterfowl population in the early part of the twentieth century, they felt that something should be done to keep the duck and goose population from dropping any further. In 1916 the United States and Great Britain, on behalf of Canada, which then was governed by Great Britain, passed the Migratory Bird Treaty. The treaty was enacted to protect the more than eight hundred species of migratory birds that live

(Opposite page) Birds fly over a thriving wetland area. Ironically, conservationists and hunters alike have joined together in an attempt to preserve wetlands.

81

in the United States and Canada. It protected waterfowl by limiting the length of the hunting season. Before the Migratory Bird Treaty was signed, for example, the duck hunting season in the state of Illinois was open 225 days a year. After the treaty was put into effect, federal regulations limited the duck hunting season to 105 days a year. Limiting the hunting season slowed the waterfowl population's decline. But many hunters and conservationists understood that much more needed to be done to insure that the waterfowl population remained stable.

One important step in protecting waterfowl, conservationists realized, was to protect the wetland habitats that waterfowl need to survive. One way to assure this protection was for the government to buy the wetlands. To fund the purchase of wetland habitats for waterfowl, Congress enacted the Migratory Bird Hunting Stamp Act, commonly known as the Duck Stamp Act, in 1934. It required duck hunters to buy a stamp from the federal government to accompany their hunting license. The money collected from the sale of duck stamps was used to buy and protect wetland areas used by waterfowl. The U.S. government eventually set up over 480 national

Many species of ducks, including this canvasback, have benefited from recent legislation that curtails hunting and protects wetland habitat.

A duck hunter takes aim as his dog eagerly awaits. Duck hunters must purchase a stamp that allows them to hunt legally. Monies from the stamps are used to preserve wetlands.

wildlife refuges, which contained more than ninety million acres of land. Many of these wildlife refuges contain wetland areas that are used by waterfowl such as ducks and geese for nesting, feeding, and wintering sites.

The Ramsar Convention

Conservationists have also worked for government protection of wetlands on a worldwide scale. The Convention of Wetlands of International Importance Especially as Waterfowl Habitat—known as the Ramsar Convention because of its adoption in Ramsar, Iran, in 1971—was the first major worldwide effort to protect wetlands. The treaty that resulted from this meeting provides for international cooperation in protecting wetlands

People enjoy a wildlife sanctuary that includes a wetland area. Many such areas have been set aside with the help of laws that protect them.

from development and pollution. More than seventy countries, including the United States, are now members of the Ramsar Convention.

The Ramsar Convention has no legal power to enforce wetland conservation; rather, there is a general obligation for members to include wetland conservation in their natural resource planning policies and promote the conservation and wise use of wetlands within their territories. Delegates from member countries meet every three years. They evaluate Ramsar wetland sites, discuss progress in wetland conservation, and make decisions on the direction of future conservation efforts.

Once a wetland in a member nation is placed under the protection of the Ramsar treaty, that nation's government promises to insure that any commercial use that is made of the wetland must not harm its ecosystem. At least one wetland area in each nation must be designated for the convention's "List of Wetlands of International Importance." Wetlands are selected as a Ramsar site because they are particularly good examples of a specific type of wetland in their region. Factors such as the importance and rarity of the animals and plants that live in a wetland are evaluated, as well as the wetland area itself. So far, nearly six hundred wetland sites that include eighty-eight million acres of wetland area are on the Ramsar Convention's list. One such wetland is Kakadu National Park in the Northern Territory of Australia. The 335,700-acre park is made up of a wide variety of wetland types. Kakadu National Park is home to up to three million waterbirds, mostly geese and ducks. The park includes 363,000 acres of seasonally flooded grasslands and swamps that support at least 225 species of freshwater wetland plants. Kakadu National Park also includes a 225-square-mile coastal mangrove swamp, which is home to fish, turtles, crocodiles, and many other saltwater reptiles and amphibians.

The Clean Water Act

In the United States many conservationists view federal regulation as one of the best ways of stopping wetland destruction. In the past few decades millions of acres of wetlands have been put under federal protection. But wetlands are still disappearing at an alarming rate. About two hundred thousand to three hundred thousand acres of wetlands are destroyed every year. So now, while conservationists are still working to put more wetlands under federal protection, they are equally concerned about the lack of enforcement action against those who destroy wetlands that are already under protection.

The Clean Water Act, passed in 1972, and a farm bill that was passed in 1985 both include provisions for protecting wetlands and enforcing wetland protection policies. Section 404 of the

Clean Water Act forbids the filling, dredging, and polluting of wetlands unless permission is given by the U.S. Army Corps of Engineers. It also gives the Environmental Protection Agency (EPA) authority to set guidelines for the circumstances under which such permits can be issued.

The application and enforcement of the Clean Water Act has not been as simple as it first appeared. While some wetland areas were saved, far more were destroyed. The vague and unclear language in the Clean Water Act caused the Corps of Engineers to have many disagreements with the EPA over which areas should be considered wetlands and what kinds of activities constitute filling wetlands or polluting them. Section 404 of the Clean Water Act includes no provision to halt

Conservationists have urged federal protection for more wetlands in hopes of protecting habitat for wildlife such as the egret.

flooding or removal of native plants from wetland areas—all of which can be just as destructive as polluting, draining, and filling.

Destruction continues

Another part of the problem is that different agencies have different interpretations of the Clean Water Act. The EPA and many federal judges consider the act to be a broad mandate to protect wetland resources. But the Corps of Engineers has continued to issue thousands of permits a year for their destruction. In 1992 the Corps of Engineers was called on to make decisions on over sixteen thousand permit applications for filling wetlands. Out of those sixteen thousand permit applications, only four hundred were turned down.

Just as lack of clarity and agreement on wetland uses have weakened protection policies, lack of funding has significantly hindered enforcement efforts. Environmental writer George Laycock says, in a July 1990 article in *Audubon*, "For example, the field office responsible for checking wetlands permits over one Ohio Valley area, with a radius of perhaps one hundred miles in parts of three states, consists of one man and an answering machine." Because of these problems, the Clean Water Act has had little effect on the rapid pace of the nation's wetland loss.

A new approach

Congress tried a different approach to wetland protection in 1985 when it passed what came to be known as the "swampbuster amendment." The amendment, part of a general farm bill, states that federal farm program benefits would be taken away from farmers who drained wetlands on their property.

Opinions are mixed on the benefits of this approach. Farmers feel like they are being unfairly singled out for harsh treatment. Conservationists wonder whether the amendment will achieve its goals. Roger L. DiSilvestro, former senior editor of *Audubon* magazine, says:

> The Fish and Wildlife Service hopes the amendment will help protect some 5 million acres of wetlands in the lower forty-eight states, including prairie potholes and lower Mississippi Valley bottomlands. There is little doubt, however, that in highly productive agricultural areas the swampbuster amendment alone will not be enough to stop unnecessary drainage.

Property rights

Wetland protection laws have come under fire from several groups. Those who have been or will be prevented from using or developing their land because it contains wetlands oppose such limits. Farmers and other landowners, real estate developers, and even some city governments are among those who have opposed some wetland protection measures.

One of the concerns voiced by these groups is that past government policies encouraged and even helped farmers and others drain and develop wetland areas. All across the country crops now grow on land that was once wetlands, and urban and commercial development have also gone forward. Under more recent policies some farmers are being asked to stop planting crops in former wetland areas to allow restoration of those wetlands. This has led to much anger and confusion. Lawrence Kropp, a farmer in North Dakota, says:

> If you'd come here 40 years ago, half our land would have been classified as wetlands. The government did all the engineering. They advised us how to drain the land. They wanted us to do it. What these people don't seem to realize is that the land they say we should take out of production is the same land that gives them cheap food.

Under the Swampbuster amendment, farmers lose their federal farm program benefits if they drain off or otherwise destroy wetlands on their property. Farmers protest this invasion of their property rights, even though much farmland, such as this farm surrounding the Missouri River, may have acres of wetlands.

In the past several years property rights advocates have grouped themselves into hundreds of organizations that work against many EPA, state, and local environmental regulations, including those that regulate wetland use. The majority of these groups started in the mid-1980s, when an increasing number of environmental laws that regulated the use of private property were passed. Until that time, most environmental laws were focused on large industries that were dumping huge amounts of toxins into the environment. Farmers, loggers, miners, oil and gas producers, and land developers, who are affected by many of the new environmental protection laws, are among the movement's biggest supporters.

They believe that if the government prohibits them from using part of their income-producing property, it should be required to offer fair financial compensation. This is especially true when land that has been farmed or used for other income-producing purposes for years—even for generations—is suddenly considered to be protected when a new definition of *wetland* is adopted. The property rights movement would like to curtail some environmental regulations and force the government to pay a fair sum for land that can no longer be used for income-producing activities. In the March 14, 1994 issue of *U.S. News & World Report*, Donald Schmitz, a member of the property rights group Fifth Amendment Foundation, says: "It would cool [the government's] jets significantly if it had to pay people for what it stole."

Private rights versus public good

There is still much discussion about how far government agencies should go in the private-property-rights-against-public-good debate. Land use cases involving wetlands and other environmental issues are awaiting hearings at all levels of the justice system—from the Supreme Court down to state and local courts. With so many issues involved, the conflict is likely to continue for some time. Betsy Carpenter writes in an article in *U.S. News & World Report:*

> Ultimately, the controversy between land rights activists and environmentalists boils down to the perennial [enduring] question of how to balance private rights with public good. Though the basic question has remained the same since the colonial era, circumstances have changed—and greatly. Scientists now have a much richer understanding of how countless small assaults on the part of millions of individuals can threaten a region's ecological health.

Environmental groups work for wetlands conservation

Despite all that is being done to prevent wetlands from being destroyed, wetland loss remains a serious problem. This is why many environmental groups make saving wetland ecosystems one of their most important goals. Many endangered species of plants and animals live in or around wetlands. Environmentalists believe that the uniqueness and diversity of life found in wetland ecosystems warrants the highest level of protection possible. Several approaches are currently being taken by environmental groups to help save wetlands.

Some environmental organizations are buying wetland areas to make sure they are not destroyed and can remain in their natural state. The Nature Conservancy, for example, has bought and protected over 6.5 million acres of wetland areas, ranging in size from one-quarter acre to hundreds of square miles. One wetland area protected by the Nature Conservancy is the sixteen-hundred-acre Jepson Preserve, located in California's Central Valley. Sixty-nine species of plants that can

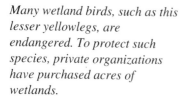

Many wetland birds, such as this lesser yellowlegs, are endangered. To protect such species, private organizations have purchased acres of wetlands.

be found only in California, including several on the endangered list, live in the Jepson Preserve. The preserve is also home to numerous endangered animals, including the tadpole shrimp, the delta green ground beetle and the California tiger salamander.

Other organizations, such as Ducks Unlimited, Inc., raise money for wetland protection. Ducks Unlimited has been working to protect wetland habitats for waterfowl for over fifty years. The organization was founded in Canada by a group of hunters who were concerned about the loss of wetland habitats for waterfowl. It is now recognized as the world's largest private wetland conservation organization. Since the group's inception in 1937, Ducks Unlimited has raised over

$490 million, which has been used to protect wetland waterfowl habitats in Canada, the United States, and Mexico. In addition to waterfowl, over six hundred species of wildlife live or feed in wetlands protected by Ducks Unlimited. Species that benefit from these protected wetlands include endangered animals such as the bald eagle, whooping crane, and the peregrine falcon.

Rebuilding the waterfowl population

Ducks Unlimited also works with federal, state, and local government agencies, as well as other conservation groups, to find ways to best protect and restore damaged wetland areas. Ducks Unlimited, along with Wildlife Habitat Canada and other conservation and government groups, helped formulate the North American Waterfowl Management Plan. This fifteen-year agreement among the governments of Canada, the United States, and Mexico took effect on May 14, 1986. It establishes goals for rebuilding North America's waterfowl population by protecting over six million acres of wetlands. The plan focuses on the importance of maintaining enough high-quality wetland habitats to ensure the abundance of ducks, geese, and swans.

In order for this plan to be fully effective, private organizations and government agencies will need to raise $1.5 billion in funds by the year 2000. The North American Waterfowl Management Plan calls for government agencies, as well as private conservation groups, to cooperate more fully on waterfowl management than they have in the past. Roger L. DiSilvestro, former senior editor of *Audubon* magazine, says:

> Effective implementation will require that agriculturalists put waterfowl conservation before profit . . . and that wildlife biologists in the United

States and Canada put management needs before jurisdictional jealousies. The success of this plan will be a measure of U.S. and Canadian commitment to wildlife conservation.

The future of wetlands

Even after all that has been done to protect them, the future of many wetlands is still uncertain. For every acre of wetland that is saved through the work of conservation groups and legislation, many more are lost through ignorance or willful destruction. Helping the public learn about the value of wetland ecosystems is an important part of wetland protection efforts. Public opinion can make a difference in national, state, and local wetland policy. In a July 1990 article in *Audubon*, environmental writer Peter Steinhart says:

> There is no Wilderness Act or Wild and Scenic River Act for wetlands, but a patchwork of laws.

The North American Waterfowl Management Plan, involving Canada, the United States, and Mexico, is an attempt to reach agreement and share resources to protect endangered wetland wildlife, including the Trumpeter Swan and the Canadian goose.

We are piecemeal in our approach to wetlands because we are piecemeal in our attitudes. Wetlands tug at both sides of our minds. We know how valuable wetlands are. But then, their slurping mud and obscure life-forms suck and hiss at our imaginations.

Much remains to be done before the world's wetlands, and the plants and animals that live there, can be considered out of danger. But people who value wetlands hope that the combined efforts of government and private organizations will preserve remaining wetlands and restore many of the wetland areas that have been damaged through centuries of misuse and misunderstanding.

Glossary

amphibian: Cold-blooded vertebrates such as frogs, toads, and salamanders that have characteristics of both fishes and reptiles.

biodiverse: Biological variety of plant and animal species in an environment.

bog: A wetland area that has spongy ground that is covered mostly by sphagnum moss.

brackish: Water that is slightly salty.

cattail: A grasslike plant that grows in many wetlands.

ecological niche: The place a plant or animal species has in the food chain of an ecosystem.

ecosystem: The plants, animals, and other organisms and their habitat that make up a functioning ecological system.

estivation: A prolonged light sleep; a form of hibernation.

estuary: A salty or brackish wetland located in coastal bays and where the mouth of a river meets the ocean; also estuarine.

floodplain: Land along a river or stream that floods at regular intervals.

habitat: The environment where plants, animals, and other organisms live.

hydric soil: Soil that has been soaked underwater for long periods.

mangrove: A species of tree that has long, stiltlike roots and grows in tropical and subtropical swamps.

marsh: A shallow wetland dominated by cattails, reeds, and similar types of nonwoody plants.

microorganism: An organism of microscopic size.

nitrate: A chemical commonly used in fertilizer.

peat: Partly decomposed sphagnum moss and other plant materials. Peat forms in bogs after dead plant materials have spent long periods of time under waterlogged conditions.

phosphorus: A chemical used in many types of commercial fertilizers.

prairie potholes: Seasonally wet depressions in the ground, which were formed by glaciers during the Ice Age. They are found in the midwestern plains of the United States and Canada.

runoff: Chemical substances, such as fertilizer, that are washed off the land and into the water supply by rain.

sphagnum moss: A moss that grows in bogs and can store large amounts of water in its cells.

swamp: A forested wetland that contains many woody trees and shrubs.

Organizations
to Contact

American Rivers

801 Pennsylvania Ave. SE, Ste. 400

Washington, DC 20003

(202) 547-6900

American Rivers is a public-interest group working to preserve and restore America's river systems and associated wetlands. Publishes *American Rivers* (quarterly) and brochures such as *American Rivers Guide to Scenic River Designations, American Rivers: Outstanding Rivers List*, and *Grassroots River Protection.*

American Wildlands

3609 S. Wadsworth Blvd., Ste. 123

Lakewood, CO 80235

(303) 988-1360

Members are individuals dedicated to the conservation of America's wildland resources. Conducts scientific and economic research of wildland resources and makes findings available to the public. Sponsors programs and forums on proper management of wetlands, watersheds, free-flowing rivers, and other wildlands. Publishes a bimonthly newsletter, *It's Time to Go Wild* and quarterly issues of *On the Wild Side* and *Wildlife Resource Economic Report.*

Association of State Wetland Managers

PO Box 2463

Berne, NY 12023

(518) 872-1804

Members are professional wetland managers and others who are interested in wetland management. Seeks to promote and improve protection and management of U.S. wetlands and foster cooperation among government agencies, environmental organizations, and the general public. Works to improve knowledge and awareness of the field. Publishes quarterly issues of *Wetland News* and various research reports.

Ducks Unlimited, Inc.
1 Waterfowl Way
Memphis, TN 38102
(901) 758-3825

Members are conservationists in the United States, Canada, and Mexico who are interested in waterfowl and wildlife habitat conservation. Ducks Unlimited works to protect and restore the wetland areas that are necessary for migrating waterfowl in North America. Publishes numerous brochures on waterfowl and their wetland habitats.

Environmental Protection Agency (EPA)
Office of Wetlands, Oceans, and Watersheds
401 M St. SW
Washington, DC 20460
(800) 832-7828

The EPA is an independent agency of the U.S. government. The EPA was established to research, monitor, set, and enforce national environmental standards. It works with state and local governments, as well as private conservation groups, to protect the environment from pollution and other types of damage. Publishes free fact sheets, brochures, and other publications.

Friends of the Everglades
101 Westward Dr., No. 2
Miami Springs, FL 33166
(305) 888-1230

Friends of the Everglades is made up of research scientists, professional engineers, and concerned citizens. Works to conserve the Everglades and educate the public as to how a harmonious coexistence between humans and the Everglades environment can best be achieved. Operates the Environmental Information Service to improve communication among organizations, institutions, and individuals most affected by environmental problems, and to increase public awareness and participation in environmental issues. Publishes the *EIS Newsletter* and *Environet* news journal periodically. Also publishes an annual, the *Everglades Reporter.*

National Audubon Society
950 Third Ave.
New York, NY 10022
(212) 832-3200

Grassroots environmental organization dedicated to protecting wildlife and its habitats. Maintains state and regional offices and participates in policy research, lobbying, and citizen action to protect and restore wildlife habitats, including wetlands, throughout North America. Publishes a monthly magazine, *Audubon.*

The Nature Conservancy
1815 N. Lynn St.
Arlington, VA 22209
(703) 841-5300

International organization that works to preserve plants, animals, and natural communities that represent the diversity of life on earth by protecting the lands and waters they need to survive. Manages a system of over thirteen hundred nature sanctuaries in all fifty states. Publishes a bimonthly magazine, *Nature Conservancy.*

Sierra Club
730 Polk St.
San Francisco, CA 94109
(415) 776-2211

Goals are "to explore, enjoy, and protect the wild places of the earth; to practice and promote the responsible use of the earth's ecosystems and resources; to educate and enlist humanity to protect and restore the quality of the natural and human environment; and to use all lawful means to carry out these objectives." Publishes a bimonthly magazine, *Sierra*, as well as numerous books and pamphlets.

Waterfowl U.S.A.
Box 50
Waterfowl Building
Edgefield, SC 29824
(803) 637-5767

Members are hunters, conservationists, and other people who are working to develop, preserve, restore, and maintain waterfowl habitats in the United States. They work to develop state and local wetland projects and improve resting areas for waterfowl. Publishes a bimonthly magazine, *Waterfowl*, and various brochures and pamphlets.

World Wildlife Fund (WWF)
1250 24th St. NW
Washington, DC 20037
(202) 293-4800

Works to preserve endangered species of animals and plants, as well as preserve their natural habitats. Works with public agencies, private agencies, and governments to meet conservation goals. Publishes a bimonthly newsletter, *Focus*. A catalog of books, pamphlets, and other WWF publications is available.

Suggestions for Further Reading

Lewis Buck, *Wetlands: Bogs, Marshes, and Swamps.* New York: Parents Magazine Press, 1974.

Sally Carringhar, *One Day at Teton Marsh.* Lincoln: University of Nebraska Press, 1979.

Helen J. Challand, *Disappearing Wetlands.* Chicago: Childrens Press, 1992.

Bryony Coles and John Coles, *People of the Wetlands— Bogs, Bodies, and Lake-Dwellers.* New York: Thames and Hudson, 1989.

Sheila Cowing, *Our Wild Wetlands.* New York: J. Messner, 1980.

Christopher Lynn, *The Everglades: Exploring the Unknown.* Mahwah, NJ: Troll, 1976.

Lorus J. Milne and Margery Milne, *The Mystery of the Bog Forests.* New York: Putnam, 1984.

William A. Niering, *Wetlands.* New York: Knopf, 1985.

Lynn M. Stone, *Wetlands.* Vero Beach, FL: Rourke Enterprises, 1989.

Marjory Stoneman, *The Everglades: River of Grass.* Sarasota, FL: Pineapple Press, 1988.

Michael J. Ursin, *Life in and Around Freshwater Wetlands.* New York: Thomas Y. Crowell, 1975.

Additional Works Consulted

Rudy Abramson, "Florida's Apologies to Nature," *Los Angeles Times*, February 15, 1992.

Wallace Arthur, *The Green Machine: Ecology and the Balance of Nature.* Cambridge, MA: Basil Blackwell, 1990.

Molly Garrett Bang, *Wiley and the Hairy Man.* New York: Macmillan, 1976.

Edward Barnes, "Sanctuary Under Siege," *Time*, March 29, 1993.

Jim Bencivenga, "Florida Wetlands Filter City Waste," *Christian Science Monitor*, March 5, 1992.

Sally-Jo Bowman, "All Wet in Oregon—One City's Model Solution to a Wetlands Dilemma," *Nature Conservancy*, September/October 1993.

Betsy Carpenter, "This Land Is My Land: Environmentalism Is Colliding with the Rights of Property Owners," *U.S. News & World Report*, March 14, 1994.

Archie Carr, *The Everglades.* Alexandria, VA: Time-Life Books, 1979.

Elizabeth Culotta, "Vanishing Flytraps," *Audubon*, March/April 1994.

Roger L. DiSilvestro, *The Endangered Kingdom—The Struggle to Save America's Wildlife.* New York: John Wiley & Sons, 1989.

Patrick Dugan, ed., *Wetlands in Danger: A World Conservation Atlas.* New York: Oxford University Press, 1993.

Erik P. Eckholm, *Down to Earth—Environment and Human Needs.* New York: W.W. Norton, 1982.

Environmental Protection Agency staff, *America's Wetlands: Our Vital Link Between Land and Water.* Washington, DC: U.S. Environmental Protection Agency, 1988.

————, *Environmental Progress and Challenges: EPA's Update.* Washington, DC: U.S. Environmental Protection Agency, 1988.

Max Finlayson and Michael Moser, eds., *Wetlands.* New York: Facts on File, 1991.

JoAnn C. Gutin, "The Secret Life of Vernal Pools," *Nature Conservancy*, July/August 1993.

Gordon Harrison, *Mosquitoes, Malaria, and Man: A History of the Hostilities Since 1880.* New York: E. P. Dutton, 1978.

Marguerite Holloway, "Nurturing Nature," *Scientific American*, April 1994.

Jon A. Kusler, William J. Mitsch, and Joseph S. Larson, "Wetlands," *Scientific American*, January 1994.

George Laycock, "How to Save a Wetland," *Audubon*, July 1990.

Marc Lecard, "Gather No Moss?" *Sierra*, May/June 1993.

John Madison, "Some Small Blue Places," *Audubon*, July 1990.

John McPhee, *The Control of Nature.* New York: Farrar, Straus & Giroux, 1989.

G. Tyler Miller Jr., *Living in the Environment.* 2nd ed. Belmont, CA: Wadsworth Publishing, 1989.

Joanna M. Miller, "Tide Turning in Favor of Saving Wetlands," *Los Angeles Times*, August 16, 1992.

John G. Mitchell, "Our Disappearing Wetlands," *National Geographic*, October 1992.

Eugene P. Odum, *Ecology and Our Endangered Life Support Systems.* Sunderland, MA: Sinauer Associates, 1989.

George Reiger, "Symbols of the Marsh," *Audubon*, July 1990.

Jack Rudloe, *The Wilderness Coast: Adventures of a Gulf Coast Naturalist.* New York: Truman Talley Books, 1988.

Franklin Russell and editors of Time-Life Books, *The Okefenokee Swamp.* New York: Time-Life Books, 1973.

Donald G. Schueler, "Losing Louisiana," *Audubon*, July 1990.

Marlise Simons, "Dutch Do the Unthinkable: Sea Is Let In," *The New York Times*, March 7, 1993.

Bjorn Sletto, "Prairie Potholes," *Earth*, May 1994.

Peter Steinhart, "No Net Loss," *Audubon*, July 1990.

Bill Thomas, *The Swamp.* New York: W.W. Norton, 1976.

Jonathan Tolman, "The Dry Facts About Wetlands," *The Wall Street Journal*, August 25, 1994.

John Zelazny and J. Scott Feierabend, *Status Report on Our Nation's Wetlands.* Washington, DC: National Wildlife Federation, 1987.

John Zelazny and J. Scott Feierabend, eds., *Wetlands— Increasing Our Wetland Resources.* Washington, DC: National Wildlife Federation, 1988.

Index

About the Author

Anita Louise McCormick has been a freelance writer since 1987. This is her fourth book. Anita's previous books are *Space Exploration* (Lucent Books), *Shortwave Radio Listening for Beginners* (TAB/McGraw-Hill), and *The Shortwave Listener's Q and A Book* (TAB/McGraw-Hill). She has also written articles and short stories for over three dozen magazines and newspapers. Anita is a ham radio operator, shortwave listener, artist, and environmentalist, and is active on the America Online computer service. Anita was recently selected to be listed in a 1994 edition of *Contemporary Authors* (Gale Research), a series of books that lists the accomplishments of American writers.

Picture Credits